The Many Meanings
of LOVE

THE MANY MEANINGS
OF
LOVE

IN BEAUTIFUL WORDS
AND PHOTOGRAPHS

Hallmark Editions

Selected by Robert A. Wood and Barbara Loots.

The publisher wishes to thank those who have given their kind permission to reprint material included in this book. Every effort has been made to give proper acknowledgments. Any omissions or errors are deeply regretted, and the publisher, upon notification, will be pleased to make necessary corrections in subsequent editions.

Acknowledgments: John 15:13, 1 John 4:16 and Solomon 2:13 from the *King James Version Bible*. Reprinted by permission of the Cambridge University Press. Published by the Syndics of Cambridge University Press. Four lines from "Your Kisses" from *Poems* by Arthur Symons. Reprinted by permission of the publishers, Dodd, Mead & Company and William Heinemann, Ltd. "Love does not consist..." from *Wind, Sand and Stars* by Antoine de Saint-Exupéry. Copyright, 1939, by Antoine de Saint-Exupéry, copyright, 1967, by Lewis Galantiere. Reprinted by permission of Harcourt Brace Jovanovich, Inc. and William Heinemann, Ltd. "There are many kinds of love..." from *The Stillmeadow Road* by Gladys Taber. Copyright © 1962 by Gladys Taber. Reprinted by permission of J. B. Lippincott Company and Brandt & Brandt. Three-line excerpt from *Stray Birds* by Rabindranath Tagore. Reprinted with permission of Macmillan Publishing Co., Inc. Trustees of the Tagore Estate and Macmillan London and Basingstoke. Copyright 1916 by Macmillan Publishing Co., Inc., renewed 1944 by Rathindranath Tagore. Excerpt by Francis Kilvert from *Kilvert's Diary,* edited by William Plomer. Copyright 1944 by T. Perceval Smith, renewed 1972 by William Plomer. Reprinted by permission of Macmillan Publishing Co., Inc., Mr. F. R. Fletcher, the editor and Jonathan Cape, Ltd. "When I wait for your face..." by Edwin Markham. Reprinted by permission of Mrs. Virgil Markham. "We have a great vocabulary..." by Betty Dederich from *Please Touch* by Jane Howard. Copyright © 1970 by Jane Howard. Reprinted by permission of the publisher, McGraw-Hill Book Company, Inc. Excerpt by Hermann Hesse from *Siddhartha,* translated by Hilda Rosner. Copyright 1951 by New Directions Publishing Corporation. Reprinted by permission of New Directions Publishing Corporation and Peter Owen, Ltd. "Let me lose a locket..." by Gladys McKee. First published in *McCall's* Magazine. Reprinted by permission of the author. Excerpt from *Autumn Love Song* by Jesse Stuart. © 1971 Hallmark Cards, Inc. Excerpt from *My Religion* by Helen Keller. Reprinted by permission of the publisher, Swedenborg Foundation, Inc.

Love is a short word

but it contains everything.

GUY DE MAUPASSANT

LOVE (luv) 1. [*verb*] To experience profound affection; to be in love. 2. [*noun*] That disposition or state of mind wherein one person is sensitive to the attractive qualities and secret sympathies of another, and holds that person in warm and tender regard. As in...

I do love you...
as the dew loves the flowers;
as the birds love the sunshine;
as the wavelets love the breeze....

MARK TWAIN

Love hath a language of his own —
A voice that goes
From heart to heart —
whose mystic tone
Love only knows.

THOMAS MOORE

To love you
        is to love the trees,
is to love the warm
        and gentle breeze,
is to love the world I see.
To love you
        is to love the days,
is to love the morning's
        warming rays
and the night's tranquility.
To love you
        is to love to live,
is to love to share
        and care and give,
and it's wanting to be me…
To love you.

MARY WALLEY

It is difficult to define love.
But we may say that in the soul,
                    it is a ruling passion;
in the mind, it is a close sympathy
                    and affinity;
          in the body, a wholly secret
               and delicate longing to possess
what we love — and this
               after much mystery.

LA ROCHEFOUCAULD

I love you for the sake
               of what you are,
And not of what you do.

JEAN INGELOW

7

LOVE (luv) 3. [*verb*] To embrace, to kiss, to pay amorous attention with flattery, small kindnesses, and general solicitude for the loved person. 4. [*noun*] Desire, physical attraction. As in...

I send you a cream white rosebud
With a flush on its petal tips;
For the love that is purest
and sweetest
Has a kiss of desire on the lips.

JOHN BOYLE O'REILLY

Did I love thee? I only did desire
To hold thy body unto mine,
And smite it with strange fire
Of kisses burning as a wine.

GEORGE MOORE

8

Sweet, can I sing you
*   the song of your kisses?*
How soft is this one,
*   how subtle this is…*
And this through laughter,
*   and that through weeping*
Swims to the brim
*   where Love lies sleeping.*

ARTHUR SYMONS

A glance, a smile,
*   or the clasp of hands,*
The kind of heart that understands,
A name soft spoken, a lingered kiss —
The price of love is paid in this.

MARY DAWSON HUGHES

To love I must have something
I can put my arms around.

HENRY WARD BEECHER

The briefest glance…
the slightest touch
to those in love
can say so much…
The highest heights
two hearts can reach
come wordless…come through
silent speech.

BARBARA BURROW

LOVE (luv) 5. [*noun*] A lover's agitated state of mind;
feelings of elation; attitude popularly regarded as a
kind of sickness. As in...

Love is the magician,
the enchanter, that changes
worthless things to joy....
With it, earth is heaven
and we are gods.

R. G. INGERSOLL

Love sets the heart
aching so delicately
there's no taking a wink of sleep
for the pleasure
of the pain.

GEORGE COLEMAN

Life is a peaceful walk
    through quiet meadows,
    a song of joy, a sun-kissed morning,
      a star-swept sky,
  a new world dawning…
    when you're in love.

BARBARA PLUMB

I wear your love and they say it shows.

NANCY BAKER SMITH

Love is the most fun
    you can have without laughing.

OLD ADAGE

At the very touch of love
everyone becomes a poet.

PLATO

I wish you always
in your heart
like the chime of silver bells
the rapture and the rhapsody
of love, whose music gives meaning
to the rhythm of life.

KAY WISSINGER

Love is a hundred lives.

JESSE STUART

LOVE (luv) 6. [*noun*] The person who is the object of affection; a term of endearment applied to the beloved. As in...

Sunlight reminds me of thee, love,
So sunny is joy when we meet.

AUTHOR UNKNOWN

O, my luve's like a red, red rose
That's newly sprung in June.

ROBERT BURNS

O love, my world is you!

CHRISTINA ROSSETTI

Come live with me
and be my love,
And we will all
the pleasures prove
That valleys, groves,
or hills, or fields,
Or woods and steepy
mountains yields.

CHRISTOPHER MARLOWE

Men always want to be
a woman's first love —
women like to be
a man's last romance.

OSCAR WILDE

But, soft! What light
through yonder window breaks?
It is the east, and Juliet is the sun...
It is my lady;
O, it is my love!

ROMEO

Arise, my love,
my fair one, and come away.

SONG OF SOLOMON

Ah, love, let us be true
To one another!

MATTHEW ARNOLD

LOVE (luv) 7. *[noun]* Love, spiritual; that mutual experience of ideas, feelings, thoughts and emotions that satisfies the deepest needs of two people in overcoming their separateness. As in...

Love does not consist
in gazing at each other
but in looking outward together
in the same direction.

ANTOINE DE SAINT–EXUPÉRY

Life is the love that reaches out,
building bridges across
gulfs of uncertainty...
to touch hands, hearts and souls
in the experience of union.

PETER SEYMOUR

True love's the gift which God has given
To man alone beneath the heaven:
The silver link, the silken tie,
Which heart to heart and mind to mind
In body and in soul can bind.

SIR WALTER SCOTT

Yours is a little love
Compared to that great force
In which all lesser loves
Have all their root and source.

But your love is near
And whispers to my heart
Of that infinite love,
Of which it is a part.

CLARA AIKEN SPEER

Love is something eternal — the aspect
may change, but not the essence.

VINCENT VAN GOGH

Love much. Earth has enough
           of bitter in it.
Cast sweets into its cup
           whene'er you can.
No heart so hard but love at last
           may win it…
Love on, through doubt and darkness;
           and believe
There is no thing which love
           may not achieve.

ELLA WHEELER WILCOX

LOVE (luv) 8. |*noun*| In religious use, that affection and paternal benevolence of God towards his children, and the reverent devotion due to God from his children. As in...

God is love;
and he that dwelleth in love,
dwelleth in God.

I JOHN 4: 16

Where there is faith, there is love.
Where there is love,
there is peace.
Where there is peace, there is God.
Where there is God,
there is no need.

MARY DAWSON HUGHES

24

God is the presence, warm,
all-enfolding, touching the drab world
into brilliance, lifting the sad heart
into song, indescribable,

beyond understanding, yet
by a bird's note, a chord of music,
a light at sunset, a sudden movement
of rapt insight, a touch of love,

making the whole universe
a safe home for the soul.

AN EARLY CHRISTIAN MYSTIC

He who loves best his fellowman
Is loving God the holiest way he can.

ALICE CARY

God is love, and He lives everywhere
there is love.

BARBARA BURROW

He loves each one of us,
as if there were only one of us.

SAINT AUGUSTINE

Sing out with joy
That all may share
The wonder
Of His love and care.

ROWENA COX

LOVE (luv) 9. [*noun*] The familial bond; the natural, protective affection between related persons. As in...

Give me no mansions,

no countries to roam,

give me a family

where love is at home.

MARY ALICE LOBERG

"Mother" and "Love"

differ only in name,

For the miracles they work

are one and the same.

KARL LAWRENCE

Where we love is home.
Home is where our feet may leave
but not our hearts.

OLIVER WENDELL HOLMES

For the evening, there is moonlight…
And for mankind, there is mother love.

HERBERT FARNHAM

Nor hell nor heaven
shall that soul surprise
Who loves the rain
And loves his home
And looks on life with quiet eyes.

FRANCES SHAW

Only a father could understand
    The special things
his children have planned.
Only a father can share, it seems,
    The vision and challenge
of loftiest dreams.

    When encouragement's needed
or questions arise,
    And you need to find someone
who's strong and wise,
    Someone who sees you
with love in his eyes,
    Only a father will do.

BARBARA BURROW

LOVE (luv) 10. [*verb*] To experience a universal sympathy among human beings; to act out of a common respect for all persons. As in ...

To unite we must love one another;
to love one another
we must know one another;
to know one another
we must meet one another.

DÉSIRÉ JOSEPH MERCIER

...I could not live
if I were alone upon the earth,
and cut off from the love
of my fellow creatures.

SYDNEY SMITH

It is only important
to love the world…
to regard the world
and ourselves and all beings
with love, admiration
and respect.

HERMANN HESSE

Kindness in words
creates confidence;
kindness in thinking
creates profoundness;
kindness in giving
creates love.

LAO-TSE

We have a great vocabulary
for hostility,
but we need new ways
to say "I love you."
Receiving affection
throws people into
more of a crisis
than being yelled at.
People need both.
It's the sound
of two hands clapping.

BETTY DEDERICH

LOVE (luv) 11. [*noun*] Friendship; the exchange of trust and affection between one person and another. As in...

The whole fruit of friendship
is in the love itself,
for it is not the advantage,
procured through a friend,
but his love itself
that gives delight.

MARCUS TULLIUS CICERO

I treasure the love of a friend
more than myself, for it is truly said,
"When a friend asks,
there is no tomorrow."

MARY DAWSON HUGHES

Greater love hath no man than this,
that a man lay down his life
for his friends.

JOHN 15: 13

Life is to be fortified
by many friendships.
To love, and to be loved,
is the greatest happiness.

SYDNEY SMITH

Love, to endure life's sorrow
and earth's woe,
Needs friendship's
solid masonry below.

ELLA WHEELER WILCOX

Let me lose a locket,
*   Money or my keys,*
And I can always find a way
*   To substitute for these;*
Let me lose a yard of time,
*   And I can race the sun,*
Or stay up till the last pale star
*   And get things done;*
But let me lose a friend I love,
*   Heart has no door nor pane,*
And all the bitter winds rush in
*   And all the lonely rain.*

GLADYS McKEE

LOVE (luv) 12. [*verb*] To enjoy deeply; to take delight in, or feel appreciation for, the attributes of some person, place or experience. As in...

My heart beats her waves at the shore
of the world and writes upon it
her signature in tears with the words
"I love thee."

RABINDRANATH TAGORE

There is no company
like the grand solemn beautiful hills.
They fascinate and grow upon us,
and one has a feeling
and a love for them
which one has for nothing else.

FRANCIS KILVERT

That the sky is brighter than the earth
means little unless the earth itself
is appreciated and enjoyed.
Its beauty loved gives the right
to aspire to the radiance
of the sunrise and the stars.

HELEN KELLER

On that beach
where time with you
was love
we kissed the day to sleep
and spoke of all our lives
as night happened
slowly above us
filling our sea with stars.

EDWARD CUNNINGHAM

When I wait for your face
      In some garden apart,
Little songs of your grace
      Carol into my heart.

When I hear the loved sound
      Of your feet that delay,
I am lifted and crowned
      On the peaks of the day.

EDWIN MARKHAM

A simple, fireside thing,
      whose quiet smile
Can warm earth's poorest hovel
      to a home…
      Such is true Love.

JAMES RUSSELL LOWELL

There are many kinds
of love, in fact,
I recently read a category of them.
But I think it is better to love
than to analyze.

GLADYS TABER

Bee
Love you
Dean